To Our Young
Snowboarder—
Love,
Mom & Dad

MORRISON

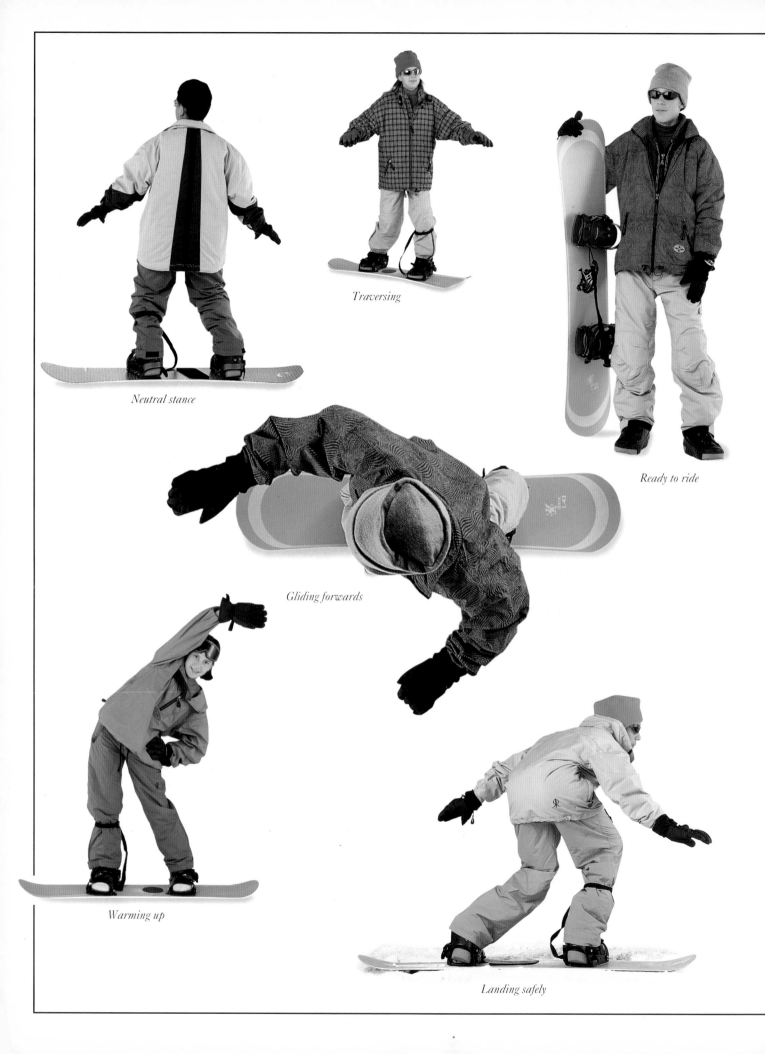

Neutral stance

Traversing

Ready to ride

Gliding forwards

Warming up

Landing safely

Toolkit

Board waxes

THE YOUNG
SNOWBOARDER

BRYAN IGUCHI

Kitting up

Getting to your feet

Racing

Falling backwards

Running flat

DORLING KINDERSLEY
London • New York • Stuttgart • Moscow

A DORLING KINDERSLEY BOOK

Project Editor Stella Love   **Art Editor** Lesley Betts
Designer Sarah Cowley
Consultant Steve Davis
Photography James Jackson
Picture Research Neil Armstrong
Production Josie Alabaster
Managing Editor Jane Yorke
Managing Art Editor Chris Scollen

The young snowboarders
Tariq Alatas, Kate Blackshaw, Rachel Davis,
Ryan Davis, Arash Hamrahian

First published in Great Britain in 1997
by Dorling Kindersley Limited
9 Henrietta Street, London WC2E 8PS

Visit us on the World Wide Web at http://www.dk.com

A CIP catalogue record for this book is available from the British Library.

ISBN 0-7513-5610-7

Colour reproduction by Colourscan, Singapore
Printed and bound in Italy by L.E.G.O.

Contents

8
To all young snowboarders

9
History of snowboarding

10
Getting ready

12
Starting out

14
Riding for a fall

16
Warming up

18
On the move

20
Traverse and run

22
First turns

24
Linking turns

26
Carving turns

28
Ground tricks and spins

30
Tricks in the air

32
Slalom racing

34
Competitions

35
Glossary

36
Index and Useful addresses

To all young snowboarders

"My aim is to ride as much powder as possible, but I also enjoy surfing and skateboarding."

THE MOUNTAINS OFFER a special kind of peace and freedom that you just don't find anywhere else. I, like many people, have discovered that snowboarding is more than just a sport, it is a lifestyle. Dedication and patience will lead to fun days of riding with friends. Snowboarding has also taught me to respect nature and appreciate the benefits of being athletic. Through competition, I've learned to deal with fears and remain calm in tough situations. I hope snowboarding will bring as much excitement into your life as it has into mine.

Bryan Iguchi

"Riding fresh powder snow is the essence of snowboarding."

"Jumping cliffs can be fun, as long as you make sure your landing is safe! But be warned, this sort of trick is only for very experienced riders. Don't try it yourself."

"Many snowboarding tricks were first done on skateboards, like the one I am doing here. It's called a method air." ,

History of snowboarding

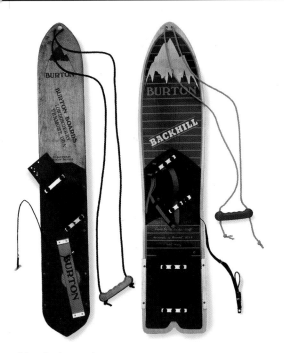

SNOWBOARDING BEGAN in the USA in the 1960s when Sherman Poppen invented the snurfer – a simple board with a rope handle attached to its nose. Snurfing as a sport was gradually taken up by a number of surf, ski, and skateboard enthusiasts who then started to improve on the idea. Jake Burton Carpenter attached rubber foot straps to boards and a former skateboard world champion, Tom Sims, also started developing new boards, experimenting with different shapes and materials. By the late 1970s, snowboarding, as it became called, was well on the way to becoming an established sport.

Early boards
One of the biggest breakthroughs in the design of early boards was made when an American, Jake Burton Carpenter, had the idea of attaching adjustable foot straps. These early bindings had a major impact on the development of the sport as they gave the rider much more control over the board and allowed longer descents to be made.

Pioneers
Tom Sims was another American pioneer of snowboarding, both in the development of boards and as a rider. In 1981, on a steel-edged board, he won the slalom title of the first snowboard championships in the USA.

Snowboarding today
Today, with media coverage of events and readily available equipment, snowboarding has become very popular. Some people are attracted by the excitement of aerial tricks or racing, others are simply keen to try their slope skills, but each year more enthusiasts are taking to snowboarding.

Freeriding fun
Freeriding is the most widespread form of snowboarding. Once the basic techniques of boarding have been mastered, the mountains are there to be explored, with a choice of runs to follow, or naturally formed bumps, jumps, and gullies to ride.

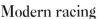

Modern racing
Racing is the speed discipline of snowboarding. A combination of skill, courage, and advances in equipment technology allows today's racers to carve their turns through the slalom gates at amazing speeds.

Freestyle
Freestyle riding incorporates all the gravity-defying tricks and spins. This style of snowboarding can be fiercely competitive, with new and daring tricks being invented all the time.

Getting ready

SNOWBOARDING is an exciting sport but, whether you plan to ride on artificial slopes or in the mountains, it is important to be properly equipped. You will need to go to specialist shops for advice on boots, boards, and bindings. They will also help you choose clothing that is practical, and right for your style of snowboarding.

You will need sunglasses or goggles with tinted lenses to protect your eyes. There are also specific tints to help you see dips and bumps in the snow on dull days.

Suncreams should always be used to protect you from sunburn and chapping in cold winds. A lip-salve will prevent your lips cracking.

What to wear

In the mountains, be prepared for changeable and extreme weather. You will need a weatherproof jacket and trousers. Wear layers of warm clothing, rather than one thick item. You can always take a layer off if you get too warm. Sunglasses or goggles are vital to protect your eyes from bright sunlight reflecting off the snow.

The leash is a safety strap to attach the board to your leg to stop it sliding away from you. It should be the first thing you put on when you reach the slopes and the last thing you take off when you leave!

Equipment shops

Go to a specialist snowboarding shop for expert and helpful advice on the equipment you need. It's a good idea to hire equipment when you first go snowboarding, until you know what you like, and what is right for you.

A freeride board is fairly wide and flexible. Racing boards are stiff and narrow by comparison.

Trousers

Your trousers need to be comfortable and loose-fitting. Look for those with extra padding around the knees and bottom to protect you when you fall!

A backpack is a good way to carry things such as spare clothing, a packed lunch, and a toolkit.

On cold days, you will need a warm hat that covers your ears. Some jackets have a useful hood tucked into the collar.

Jacket

Snowboarding jackets are expensive but you can wear them all through the winter. Look for one that is loose-fitting, comfortable, and long enough at the back to cover your bottom, and with a high neck to keep out the wind and cold.

Gloves are essential to protect your hands on dryslopes and in the snow. Some have a strap to protect your wrists from injury and a drawstring to keep the snow out.

Toolkit

It is useful to carry a small spanner and a screwdriver to adjust your bindings, and rub-on wax for your board. Wax helps the board to run well, and there are different types for the snow conditions.

Board waxes

Multi-head screwdriver

10mm spanner

Soft boots are very popular because they are comfortable and flexible.

Boots and bindings

Boots and bindings are designed to work together as a "system". There are three main types:

Step-in system

This is the newest system. The boot has a built-in metal bail screwed to its base that clicks into a spring-loaded binding as you step on to the board.

Metal bail

Lace-up step-in boot

Release lever

Soft-boot system

This is the system most people start with. It is also favoured for freestyle riding. The binding has a calf support at the back and straps to lock your foot in place.

Standard, lace-up soft boot

Toe strap

Hard-boot system

This system is best for high-speed turns and racing. The metal bails of the binding snap down on the toe and heel ridge of the hard plastic outer shell of the boots.

Hard boot with ratcheted fastenings

Heel bail *Toe bail* *Clip fastener*

Board talk

Which leg do you favour? If you prefer to lead with your left foot forwards you are a regular rider. If you prefer your right foot in front, you are riding goofy!

Most boards are similar in shape to the one below – wide at the nose and tail, but narrowing at the waist. Raceboards are longer and narrower, while freestyle boards are shorter and wider.

Regular   *Goofy*

Waist   *Nose*

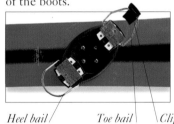

Tail

Starting out

THE FIRST FEW TIMES you clip into the bindings of your snowboard will probably feel strange. But you will soon develop a routine of checking your board and bindings, fastening the safety leash, and clipping your front foot in first. On this page you will discover some basic ways of manoeuvering on your board with just your front foot clipped in. These are basic skills but you will find that they often come in useful.

Getting on the board

Put your board across the slope, uphill from you and kneel on your back leg, facing uphill. Clip on the safety leash so that the board cannot slide away.

1 Clip the leash around your front leg and put that foot into its binding.

2 Push your heel well back into the binding and fasten the ankle strap.

3 Now fasten the toe strap. Then stand up and use the toe edge as a brake.

Step, scoot, and turn

Moving on flat ground is something you need to learn how to do. Here is a sequence of basic skills for you to try so that you can move easily on the level.

Stomp pad

Stomp pad
This is a non-slip pad next to the rear binding on which you can rest your free foot when scooting.

Turn your shoulders and upper body to face the direction of travel.

Don't look down to locate the stomp pad.

1 Start by walking the board along, taking small steps. Place your free foot close to the toes of your front foot for each step.

2 Then try scooting along. Push from your free foot to make the board glide forwards. Keep the board flat.

Safety leash

3 Aim to hold the gliding position for longer each time you scoot, and rest your free foot on the stomp pad.

Walking on the level

There will always be times when you need to unclip your back foot and take a few steps.

Drive your arms to help you move along.

Keep each step fairly small.

Slide the board along with your front foot.

1 Release your back foot from its binding and take a step with it parallel to your board.

2 Push with your free foot to slide the board forwards. Use the swing of your arms to help.

Walking uphill

Sometimes you will need to take a few steps up a slope, for example in a queue for a ski-lift.

Keep your board horizontal, across the slope.

Dig in the toe edge to stop the board sliding away from you.

1 Release your back foot and step uphill on to it, turning your board across the slope.

2 Lift the board up, digging the toe edge into the slope before you take the next step.

4 To turn the board to face a new direction, take a small step away from its toe edge, on to your free foot.

5 Tilt the board on to its toe edge, behind you. Then lift or drag it to bring the nose around your free foot.

6 Take another step into the turn and lift the board round again. Keep your steps small and your feet fairly close together.

On icy ground, turn in lots of small stages.

Take small steps with your free foot.

The toe edge of the board will give you stability, so use it to help you.

Nose

Riding for a fall

N O MATTER HOW good you become as a snowboarder, there are going to be times when you fall over. Learning how to fall will help to prevent injuries to your hands and wrists, and make those falls less jarring. Also, knowing how to get back on to your feet from your toe edge, will save you a lot of fatigue and frustration, particularly during your early lessons.

Falling backwards

If you catch a heel edge and fall backwards, try to relax, crouch, and roll.

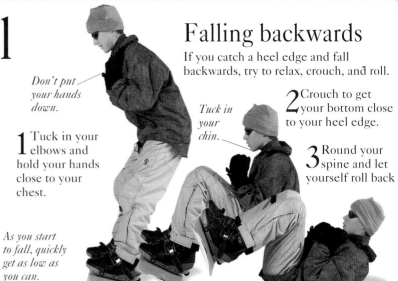

Don't put your hands down.

1 Tuck in your elbows and hold your hands close to your chest.

Tuck in your chin.

2 Crouch to get your bottom close to your heel edge.

3 Round your spine and let yourself roll back

As you start to fall, quickly get as low as you can.

Roll to absorb the impact.

Falling forwards

The important thing when falling is to keep your arms tucked in until you're on the ground. Then use your forearms to prevent your head hitting it.

2 Fall on to your knees and carry on forwards, then use your forearms to cushion the landing.

Tuck in your elbows.

1 Clench your fists and tuck in your elbows. Hold your arms into your chest.

Use your forearms, not your hands.

You can wear extra padding on your knees.

3 Get back on to you feet by walking your hands back towards the board.

Dig your toe edge in as you get back up.

Getting up toeside

It is easier to get up on your toe edge than your heel edge, so if you fall backwards, roll the board over like this.

Start to take this hand over and reach out in front of you.

Lift with your front leg, keeping the tail still.

Angle the board with your legs.

Tail

1 Sit back, resting on your hands. Keep your board tail still and use your front leg to pull the nose in towards you.

Support yourself on your hands.

2 Roll on to your side and start to lift the nose of your board. Keep the tail in the same spot on the ground.

Basic stances

There are two basic stances, or positions, you will use on your board time and time again. Both should feel natural and comfortable to hold.

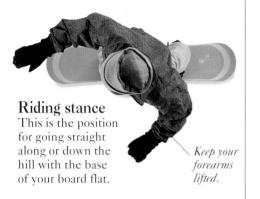

Riding stance

This is the position for going straight along or down the hill with the base of your board flat.

Keep your forearms lifted.

Keep your back straight.

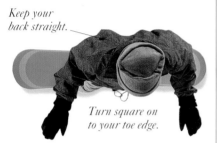

Turn square on to your toe edge.

Neutral stance

This is the position to use, with your weight evenly on both feet, for braking, or sideslipping. In other words, when using your edges to skid to a stop.

Basic riding position

Here you can see a basic riding position. Everyone will vary this position slightly to suit their own style of riding, but the principles remain the same. Basic posture is for moving forwards, so you need to look where you are going and guide your board.

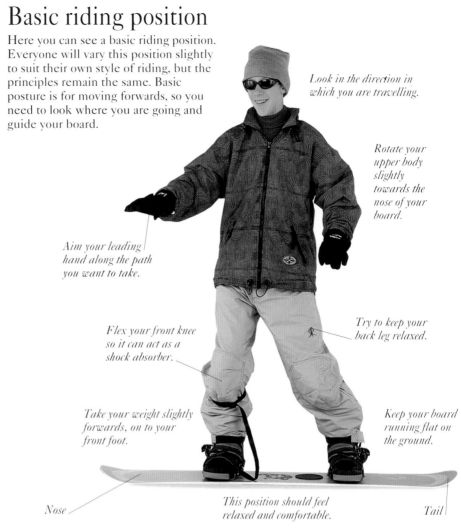

Look in the direction in which you are travelling.

Rotate your upper body slightly towards the nose of your board.

Aim your leading hand along the path you want to take.

Try to keep your back leg relaxed.

Flex your front knee so it can act as a shock absorber.

Take your weight slightly forwards, on to your front foot.

Keep your board running flat on the ground.

Nose

This position should feel relaxed and comfortable.

Tail

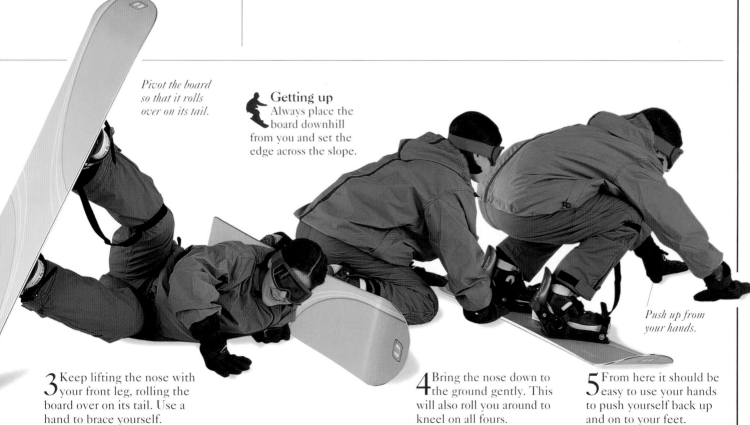

Pivot the board so that it rolls over on its tail.

Getting up
Always place the board downhill from you and set the edge across the slope.

Push up from your hands.

3 Keep lifting the nose with your front leg, rolling the board over on its tail. Use a hand to brace yourself.

4 Bring the nose down to the ground gently. This will also roll you around to kneel on all fours.

5 From here it should be easy to use your hands to push yourself back up and on to your feet.

Warming up

BEFORE YOU SET OFF, it is essential to wake up your body by warming and then stretching your muscles. Working through some warm-up exercises will increase your heartbeat and breathing rate, and loosen your muscles and joints. This will help you to avoid injury when snowboarding. It will also give you a chance to give your equipment a final check and make sure your boots and bindings are firmly fastened and comfortable.

Start with small jumps and work up to bigger ones.

Use your arms and shoulders to help you jump round.

Try to turn first one way, then the other.

Avoiding injury
Cold, stiff limbs are prone to injury. You may need to warm up again after a long cold ride to the mountain top on an exposed ski-lift.

Jump turns
Jumping up and down on the spot is a good way to get warm. Add a spin of the board and this is also a useful way to turn around.

Stretching exercises

Once you are warm from jumping up and down, or hiking up a slope carrying your board, you are ready to stretch. Before you set off, try some of these exercises.

Hot and cold
You will get warm quickly hiking uphill and riding. But beware, you can cool down equally fast when you stop for a while.

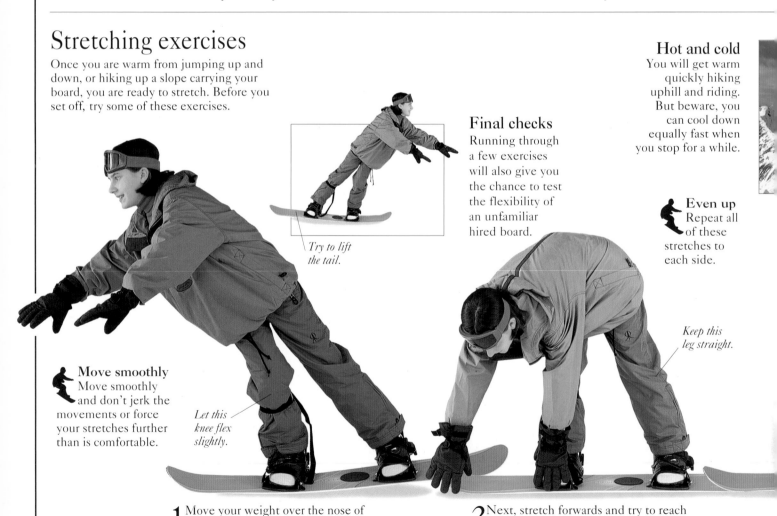

Final checks
Running through a few exercises will also give you the chance to test the flexibility of an unfamiliar hired board.

Try to lift the tail.

Even up
Repeat all of these stretches to each side.

Keep this leg straight.

Move smoothly
Move smoothly and don't jerk the movements or force your stretches further than is comfortable.

Let this knee flex slightly.

1 Move your weight over the nose of your board. Stretch as far as you can comfortably and hold it for a few seconds. Try to lift the board tail and balance. Now stretch the other way, lifting the nose.

2 Next, stretch forwards and try to reach the toe edge at the nose, and then the tail of the board. Remember to move smoothly. Only reach as far as you can and do not bounce to force the stretch further.

Exploring your edges

As a newcomer to the sport, you will find it useful to explore the edges of your board. Your edges are your braking system, so you need to know how to use them. Try rocking back and forth or balancing on them to get used to putting pressure on them.

Heel edge

Your heel edge is the edge of the board, under your heels.

Use your arms for balance.

Straighten your legs and push out your bottom.

Put pressure on to the toe edge evenly through both your legs and feet.

Bend your knees to get on to your toe edge.

Toe edge

The toe edge is the edge under your toes. Whenever you are facing uphill, you should be using your toe edge.

Breathtaking
Try to keep breathing normally through each exercise.

Keep your arms up.

Twist slowly to each side.

Make sure you bend sideways, not forwards.

Stretch up from your waist.

Support yourself with one hand on your hip.

Relax your knees. Don't lock them.

Don't worry if you cannot reach your toes.

Keep your legs straight.

3 Stretch the back of your legs by reaching down to your toes, keeping your legs straight. Just stretch and hold. Stand up again slowly, so you do not get dizzy.

4 Now work your upper body. Raise your arms as if carrying a tray, and rotate as far as you can, twisting from your waist. Hold the position, then repeat to the other side.

5 Stretch out your sides. Take one arm up over your head and bend sideways, supporting yourself by placing the opposite hand on your hip. Now you are ready to ride.

On the move

A T FIRST YOU WILL feel that your board has a mind of its own. As soon as you start to move, it slides away with you. Learn to sideslip and you will be able to keep your board firmly under control, even on the steepest of slopes. This is a skill that you can use in any tight spot.

Diagonal sidesliping

Diagonal sideslipping is like straight sideslipping but you use your weight and rotation at the same time to move diagonally across the slope. Here you can see how to sideslip on your heel edge.

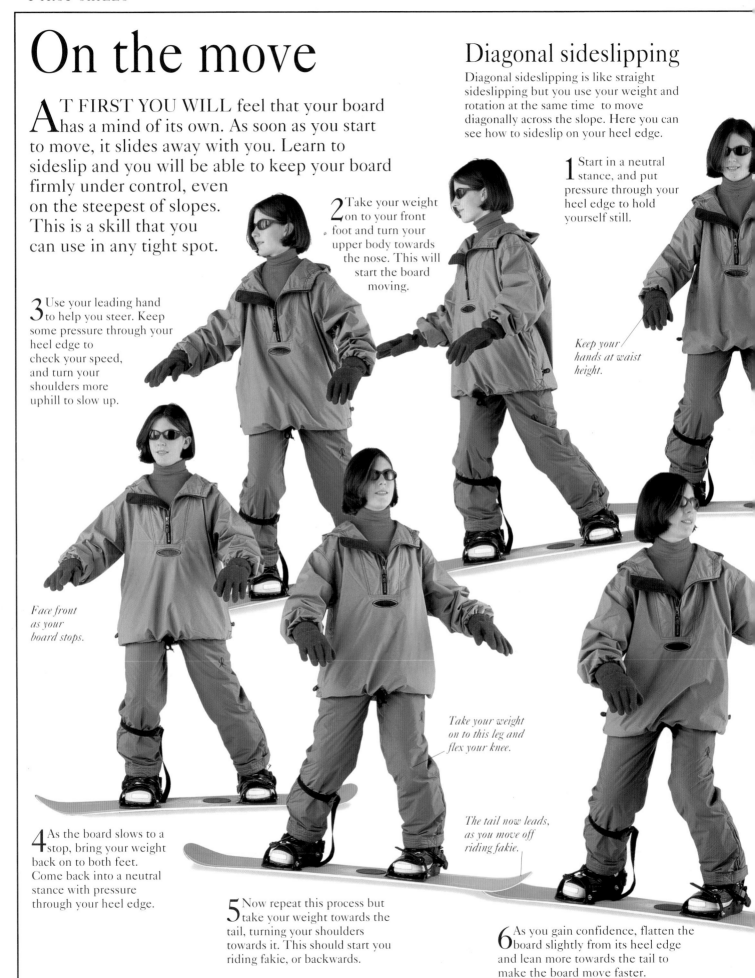

2 Take your weight on to your front foot and turn your upper body towards the nose. This will start the board moving.

3 Use your leading hand to help you steer. Keep some pressure through your heel edge to check your speed, and turn your shoulders more uphill to slow up.

1 Start in a neutral stance, and put pressure through your heel edge to hold yourself still.

Keep your hands at waist height.

Face front as your board stops.

Take your weight on to this leg and flex your knee.

4 As the board slows to a stop, bring your weight back on to both feet. Come back into a neutral stance with pressure through your heel edge.

5 Now repeat this process but take your weight towards the tail, turning your shoulders towards it. This should start you riding fakie, or backwards.

The tail now leads, as you move off riding fakie.

6 As you gain confidence, flatten the board slightly from its heel edge and lean more towards the tail to make the board move faster.

How to sideslip

Sideslipping is a controlled slide downhill, keeping your board horizontal across the slope. By alternately digging in an edge to brake and then flattening the board to slide, you can control your descent. You can do this on either the toe edge or the heel edge. Here, the technique is shown on the heel edge.

1 Start in a neutral stance, facing downhill. Dig in your heel edge so the board is still, and keep your weight evenly spread over both feet.

2 Slowly release the pressure on your heel edge and tilt the board slightly towards the toe edge. As the board flattens, you will start to slide.

3 To slow down, or stop, tilt the board back on to its heel edge. Keep tilting on and off your heel edge to sideslip slowly downhill.

Steering to stop
To steer to a stop, turn your upper body to look further uphill, keeping your weight in the direction of travel.

Going straight
On a very gentle slope, where there is a flat runout area, you can make a straight glide. In a basic riding stance, let your board run flat, pointing straight downhill. As the ground levels out, you will glide to a standstill.

Fast or slow
To go faster, steer the board more steeply down the slope by turning your shoulders and leading hand more downhill. To go slower, do the opposite.

Turn your shoulders to steer with your leading hand.

From this position you can decide whether to continue riding fakie, or change direction to ride forwards.

7 Steer the tail of the board uphill to brake by twisting your upper body and leading arm further round, over the tail.

8 Put pressure back on through your heel edge. As the board slows, resume your neutral stance, ready to move off again.

Keep your knees flexed.

Traverse and run

IN THE EARLY STAGES, one difficulty to overcome is the fear of pointing straight downhill as you turn from one edge to the other. To prepare for this, practise traversing diagonally across the slope on either edge. As you go, point your board further downhill to run, then bring it back across the slope.

Start to turn your shoulders downhill.

Lean forwards to drive the nose downhill.

Use your arms for balance and steering.

3 Rotate your upper body back uphill to slow down and keep control. Let yourself glide to a standstill.

1 Start on your toe edge. Take your weight forwards and rotate your shoulders to start the board turning slightly downhill.

Let your board run flat.

Put pressure back on to your toe edge.

2 Sink on to your front foot and steer with your leading hand. Rotate your shoulders further downhill.

Toeside traverse

Traversing is the term used for travelling diagonally across the hill. By turning your board downhill and then back across it, this exercise will help you to prepare for the next step, which is turning.

Rotate as far downhill as your confidence will allow.

Start off again from a neutral stance.

Lean towards the tail.

Start to rotate back uphill to check your speed.

Lean towards the leading end to drive the board round.

Put pressure back on the toe edge.

Flatten the board by gently taking pressure off your toe edge.

4 Now repeat the process, still on your toe edge but this time riding fakie. Take your weight towards the tail of your board to start the traverse.

Lean in to it
Always lean in the direction in which you want to travel. Look where you want to go, and keep your weight towards the leading end of your board.

5 To slow down again, turn your shoulders and arms back uphill. This will drive the nose back across the slope, and slow you down to a standstill.

Across a mountain

Traversing is not always a short slide across the slope, nor just a move for beginners. There are times when you may need to hold a traverse on one edge for a long diagonal slide to get right across, or around a mountainside.

Slowly turn your shoulders.

Keep your hands lifted.

3 Turn your shoulders to take your leading hand back uphill. This will steer the nose back across the slope to slow down.

Take pressure off the heel edge to let the board run.

1 On your heel edge, bend your front knee taking your weight forwards. This will start to point the nose downhill.

2 Steer with your leading hand, and bring the nose to point downhill. Allow the board to start running flat.

Go on to your heel edge again.

Heelside traverse

You can start with either heelside or toeside traverses, whichever you find easiest. But you will need to be comfortable on both sides before you can really progress to making turns.

Look where you are going, not down at your board.

Steer uphill with your leading hand.

Tail

Flatten the board and let it run.

Put pressure back on the heel edge.

4 Start off again across the slope, but this time riding backwards. Begin with your weight on your heel edge and lean towards the tail. Use your leading hand to help you steer.

Edging or running flat
Keep pressure on your working edge, except when you want the board to run flat to gain speed. Then return to that edge by putting pressure on it.

5 Check your speed again by rotating your leading arm and shoulders uphill, and run to a standstill, with your board across the slope.

Make all the movements smoothly, not suddenly.

First turns

NOW THAT YOU HAVE started to travel across and down the slope, it is time to start making turns. The secret to turning is learning how to use your weight to put pressure through different parts of the board. The diagram on this page will help you to understand where that pressure needs to be applied to make the board turn.

Keep your leading hand over the edge you are using.

Put pressure through your toe edge.

Nose

Tail

1 Place your board across the slope, with your weight equally on both feet, and pressure on your toe edge.

Heelside turn

The heelside turn starts on the toe edge, glides flat on the base for a moment and then finishes on the heel edge.

Flex your knees and keep low.

2 Move off slowly by taking your weight fowards on to your front foot and turning your shoulders into a riding stance.

Pressure points
The shaded areas show where you should be applying pressure to your board to make the turns.

Rise up slightly to help the board turn.

3 As the nose starts to point downhill extend your arms forwards and upwards. Take the pressure off your toe edge and let the board flatten.

4 Start to put pressure on your heel edge, through your front foot. Keep your arms high.

5 Now the new edge is across the slope, sink on to it and put pressure through it to slow you down.

The next stage will be to link heelside and toeside turns.

Falls
Don't be put off by falls, but try to remember how to fall safely. Even good riders wipe out occasionally, and sometimes spectacularly!

 **Watch your weight!**
Remember, the tail of your board will go too far round and drop downhill if you let your weight go back on it.

Toeside turn

The toeside turn starts on your heel edge, turns to run flat through the glide position and finishes on your toe edge.

Lean towards the nose of your board.

Practice area
Find a wide-open quiet area on a very gentle slope to practise your first turns. You will find it impossible to keep control on a steep gradient when you start out.

Put pressure through your heel edge.

Tail

Start low and flex your knees.

Nose

1 Start with your board across the slope, use your weight to put pressure through your heel edge, and move off slowly.

Slow movements
Make each movement slowly. Do not rush to change from one pressure point to another.

2 Lean slightly in the direction you want to go and take your weight forwards but keep the pressure on your heel edge.

Remember to keep looking the way you want to go.

Make sure your leading hand always stays over the edge you are using.

Keep your arms high until the board has come right round.

3 As the board turns downhill, straighten your legs as if to rise off the board, lifting your arms and taking them forwards.

4 Sink back into your board by flexing your knees and apply pressure forwards through the toe edge. Let the tail drift round.

5 Keep the pressure going through the toe edge to bring the board slowly back across the slope.

Keep your brakes active by flexing your knees.

Leading hands
Note that your leading hand moves to stay over the edge you are using throughout each turn.

Linking turns

NOW THE FUN can really start. Once you have mastered basic turns on both toeside and heelside, you are ready to start linking them together. This means you will be able to make your way smoothly down the slope without stopping. Be sure to get things right on a gentle slope before you move on to a steeper one.

Basic linked turns

Find an easy slope with plenty of space and start by trying to link just two or three turns together at a time.

Start to turn your shoulders and hips downhill.

Straighten your legs to help the board come round.

Let the board run flat.

Keep your hands forwards.

Look where you want to go.

Keep your weight on your toe edge.

1 Start on your toe edge, glance behind you to check that it is clear to go, and let your board start to slide slowly across the slope.

2 Increase the weight on the nose of your board and let it begin to point slightly more downhill.

3 Begin to rotate your chest and hips to face downhill. Keep your weight forwards and on your toe edge.

4 Pass your leading hand and arm over the front of the nose as the board points downhill.

Make your leading hand and foot work together, going the same way.

Keep turning to face the way you want to go.

Take your time
Don't rush to change on to the new edge but allow the board time to slide round.

Brake if necessary
Remember your brakes and use them to stop if you feel you are losing control.

Fall line

The fall line

A rolling ball takes the most direct path down a slope. This path, shown here as a dotted line, is the fall line. Being able to imagine this line will help you to choose your route down the slope and decide where to make your turns. Snowboarders need to be aware of the fall line as they control their speed by turning across it.

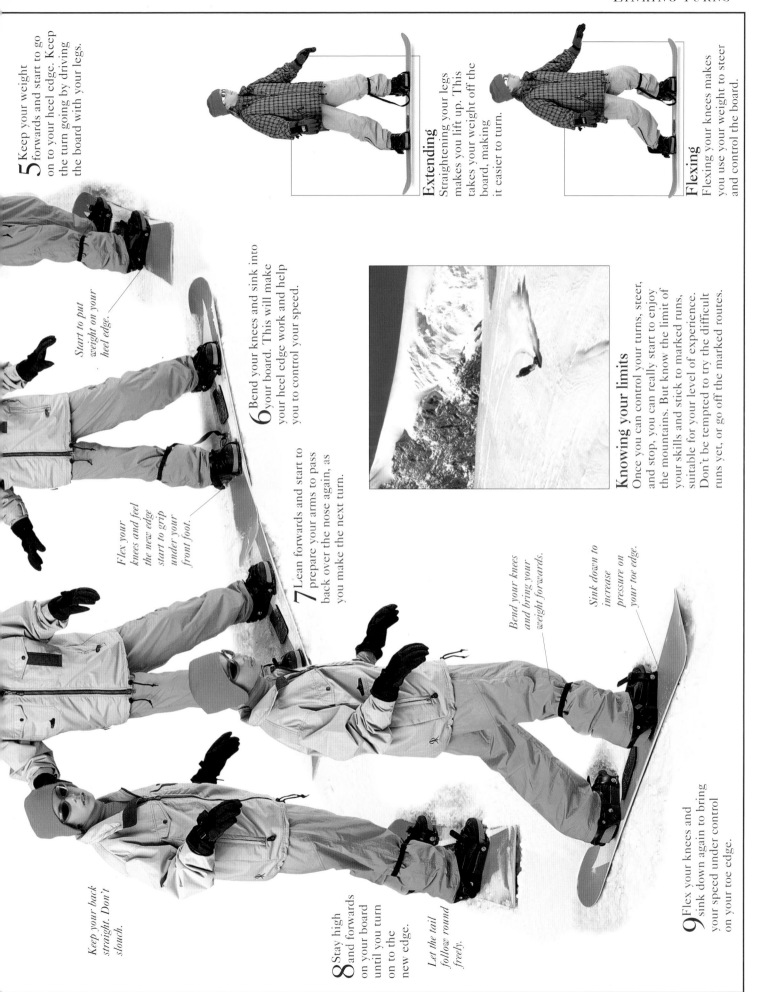

5 Keep your weight forwards and start to go on to your heel edge. Keep the turn going by driving the board with your legs.

Extending
Straightening your legs makes you lift up. This takes your weight off the board, making it easier to turn.

Flexing
Flexing your knees makes you use your weight to steer and control the board.

Start to put weight on your heel edge.

Flex your knees and feel the new edge start to grip under your front foot.

6 Bend your knees and sink into your board. This will make your heel edge work and help you to control your speed.

7 Lean forwards and start to prepare your arms to pass back over the nose again, as you make the next turn.

Knowing your limits
Once you can control your turns, steer, and stop, you can really start to enjoy the mountains. But know the limit of your skills and stick to marked runs, suitable for your level of experience. Don't be tempted to try the difficult runs yet, or go off the marked routes.

Bend your knees and bring your weight forwards.

Sink down to increase pressure on your toe edge.

Keep your back straight. Don't slouch.

8 Stay high and forwards on your board until you turn on to the new edge.

Let the tail follow round freely.

9 Flex your knees and sink down again to bring your speed under control on your toe edge.

Carving turns

PROGRESSING TO CARVED turns will really open up snowboarding for you. Carving means using the edge of the board to cut a track in the snow as you turn. The change of edge takes place earlier than on basic turns and the tail no longer slides round, slowing you down, but follows the track of the nose.

The heelside carve

The heelside carve starts on the toe edge, but you change to the heel edge before the board crosses the fall line. The curve of the board edge makes the board turn, and carve its way round.

1 Start with a fairly steep toeside traverse. This will allow you to build up the speed you need to carve your turns.

Push your weight forwards.

Start to rotate your shoulders and leading arm.

Keep your back straight.

2 Put pressure through your heel edge as you turn your head, shoulders, leading arm, and hip towards the direction of the turn.

Change on to your heel edge.

3 Sink your body weight through the heel edge by pushing your hips over the heel edge. This will make the edge grip.

Tuck your rear knee in towards your front leg.

Sink over the heel edge.

Fluid motion
As you improve, aim to change from edge to edge in a fluid, easy motion.

Keep your arms wide for stability.

4 As soon as the turn is complete, start to extend your legs. Push up from your heel edge, letting the board run flat, and prepare to link into the next toeside turn.

Making it flow
Link the rotation of your upper body, which steers your front foot, with the up and down motion of your legs and your turns will start to flow.

1 Prepare for the turn with a heelside traverse across the slope. You need to be moving to carve successfully.

Build up speed on a steep heelside traverse.

The toeside carve

The toeside carve is like the heelside turn, but starts on the heel edge. Carving turns means linking toeside and heelside turns, one after the other, to carve your way smoothly and rhythmically down the slope leaving an S-shaped track.

Start to rotate your shoulders.

Hold your arms out to help you balance.

2 As you gather speed, rotate your shoulders and arms towards the direction of the turn. Roll the board on to your toe edge.

Keep your weight forwards in the traverse position.

Roll on to your toe edge.

3 Bring your leading arm round and flex your knees to sink your body weight into your toe edge.

The amount you lean depends on the speed you are going.

Keep your back straight. Don't bend at the waist.

Look and lean into the turn.

Flex your knees and ankles.

4 Once the board crosses the fall line and has carved round, start to extend and prepare for the next heelside turn.

The edge change takes place before the board crosses the fall line.

Extreme lean
By going faster and edging the board correctly, you will find yourself leaning more into your turns, like this.

27

Ground tricks and spins

F REESTYLE RIDING is all about tricks and spins on the ground and in the air. The tricks are as varied as your imagination, and fun to try, but you will need to master your basic skills first. Learning to do nose and tail slides, spins, and riding fakie are all important skills that form the basis for many more advanced and aerial tricks.

Tail slide

The tail slide is the first stage of many tricks and spins. Once you can do a basic slide there are lots of variations to try.

Keep your back straight.

Keep it up
Aim to keep the nose in the air for longer each time you practise the tail slide.

1 Start with a straight run in a relaxed riding stance and the board running flat.

Nose slide to fakie

As you gain in skill and confidence, you may feel ready to experiment with some new moves. This nose slide includes a 180-degree spin and finishes riding fakie.

Keep your stance relaxed as you start to prepare for this trick.

Your shoulders should remain facing forwards.

Take your arms back ready to help you turn.

Use your arms to help you turn.

Flex your front knee.

Lift the tail by straightening your back leg.

Start to sink down on to your front foot.

Nose

1 From a straight run, bring all your weight on to your front leg and bend your front knee slightly.

2 Keep your shoulders facing forward but take your arms back behind you and lift the tail of the board.

Keep your head up.

Use your arms to help you balance.

Keep your front leg straight.

Flex your front leg.

2 Move your weight on to your rear foot and spread your arms out for balance.

3 Use your front leg to pull up the nose and keep your arms stretched out.

4 Keep your weight on your back foot and hold the nose in the air.

5 Take your weight forwards again to bring the nose down.

Rotation
Rotate your hips as you turn your shoulders and the board will spin round.

You are now riding fakie but still travelling in the same direction.

4 Keep the board moving until the tail has come round 180 degrees, driving it on with your back leg.

5 Your rear leg is now leading as you put the tail down on the ground. Take your weight on to it – you are now riding fakie.

Tail starts to come round to the front.

3 Keep the tail up in the air. Then, rotate your arms and upper body forwards using the movement to spin the tail of the board round.

Tail

Tricks in the air

T RICKS IN THE AIR are not just for the most daring or talented riders. Once you have mastered good basic riding techniques you will be surprised how easy some exciting looking tricks can be. Start by practising ollies, and jumps from small hits, or bumps, on the slope and gradually build up your confidence. Make sure you are aware of other slope users at all times.

Finding air
Jumps, or airs, can be turned into all sorts of exciting tricks if you have the skill and imagination. Here, you can see a heel edge grab. There are endless ways to grab your board – on either edge, by the nose or tail, or with either hand. Further variations, all with different names, can be made by boning out, or straightening one or other of your legs.

A fakie backside 180-degree indy
You will need to build up confidence and progress from straight jumps and practise spins and grabs before tackling this trick. It starts from a fakie take-off and includes a spin of 180 degrees with a grab on the toeside edge.

Safe jumping
Check that you have a clear run up to the jump and that there is a big, safe landing area, clear of rocks and people.

Take your trailing arm high to help you balance.

3 As you take off, use the forward rotation of your shoulders and arms, like a spring uncoiling, to start your spin.

Rotate your arms and shoulders, opposite to the way you are going to spin.

4 Keep your board level by spreading your weight equally. Reach down with your front arm and grab the toe edge.

Lift the tail slightly on take off. Don't let it drop.

1 Move off smoothly, riding in a confident fakie stance. Keep your head up and look forwards. Try not to look at the drop.

2 As you approach the jump, start to prepare. Flex back on to your rear leg and start to rotate your shoulders, taking your arms back.

Grab the toe edge between your feet.

Ollies

An ollie is a small jump using your own energy to take off. You can use it to go over small obstacles for fun. Practise springing up and down on the spot, taking off front foot first. Now try it on the move starting in a basic riding posture.

Hold your weight back to keep the nose rising.

Look ahead, not down.

Pull your knees up into your body.

You can land on the nose, middle or tail of the board.

Flex your knees.

1 Sink into your board and let your body weight slide towards the tail.

2 Pull up your front foot to lift the nose and spring off your back foot.

3 Keep your knees pulled up and let your weight move forwards again.

4 Straighten out to land, keeping your knees flexed to cushion the impact.

5 As you land, get your weight evenly spread so you ride off in a straight line.

5 Let go of the board in good time, and start to open out. Fix your eyes on your landing spot.

Start to spot your landing point.

6 Use a final flick of your leading hip to align the board for a straight landing.

8 As soon as you have made a good landing, and you are steady, straighten up and ride away.

7 Cushion your landing by flexing your knees, and sink down into the board to keep control.

Spread your weight evenly on the board.

A good landing and ride-off will add style to the simplest trick.

Slalom racing

RACING THROUGH THE gates of a slalom course set zig-zag down a hill is a very exciting riding style and different to that of freestyle or freeriding – it is all about speed and accuracy in a series of left and right turns. Racers use long, specially prepared boards and hard boots to gain the extra speed and fine-tuned control needed for top-level competitions. Competitions are arranged for every level and you may find it fun to take part.

Slalom technique

For this type of riding, use the edges of your board, not as brakes, but to direct the board. The less you slow down, the better. Your upper body should sweep and rotate over the nose of the board in a steady rhythm, synchronized with a pumping action from your legs. The speed of racing means that you should always wear a safety helmet.

Wear a helmet for safety.

Flex your knees to stay low.

Race wax on the base makes the board run faster.

1 Start to line up with the gate ahead. Stay low on your board and keep pressure through the toe edge.

Boot fitting
Make sure your boots fit really well so that all your movements transfer precisely to the board.

Allow the board to flatten.

2 Extend your legs slightly to start the edge change. Let the board flatten and accelerate momentarily.

Use your arms for balance.

3 Sink into your heel edge flexing your knees to get low. Widen your arms to keep your balance.

Start to look for the next gate.

4 Hold your heel edge as the nose of the board passes the gate and focus on the next gate.

Slalom gate

Top-level competition
At top level, every fraction of a second counts. Race boards are carefully prepared with special waxes and edged for maximum speed and cut. The racers wear skintight suits to cut down on air resistance and protective equipment, helmets, and arm and leg guards, to help prevent injury.

5 Rise up from the heel edge gradually to take the brakes off and increase speed.

Let your board flatten again.

6 Run flat towards the next gate and plan your line and timing for your next turn.

Leg protection
A protective guard on the leading leg reduces the chance of injury if a racer hits one of the gates.

Racing events
There are several different slalom events, such as giant slalom, and super G. They vary in the length and width of the course, but are all raced against the clock. Bordercross, shown here, is a fairly new event. It is a group race and includes all aspects of snowboarding – from slalom, to freeriding and freestyle.

7 Put your weight back on the tail to lift the nose and help you make a quicker edge change.

Drive yourself on to the finish line.

Arm protection
Cutting as close to the gates as possible, many racers push the flexible posts out of their way. For safety, riders wear arm guards.

8 Sink into your toe edge taking your weight forwards to the nose. This will control your turn, making it carve through the gate.

Get low on your toe edge.

Competitions

COMPETITIVE SNOWBOARDING is growing fast, even where there are are no snow-covered mountains. There are three competitive branches of the sport – freestyle, slalom, also called carving, and bordercross – and events are organized at every level, from local clubs, through national competitions, to international championships. You may just like to watch events and have no wish to compete but, whatever style you choose, as a snowboarder you will enjoy hours of exciting action with your friends.

Bordercross

This is a very exciting event for both spectators and participants, as it includes riders who normally race and carve and freestylers who are more at home pulling big air tricks. They race in heats of 4 to 6 competitors. Slalom-style gates set the course through banked turns called burns and it usually involves big humps and hits to negotiate, too.

Freeriding

Many snowboard enthusiasts feel that the excitement of snowboarding lies, not in competition, but in being out and about in the mountains with friends. Making flawless tracks in fresh snow, or finding natural jumps and gullies to ride, offers challenge enough without the formalities of organized events and competitions. This makes freeriding the most popular event of them all!

Halfpipe competition

A halfpipe is a U-shaped channel dug into snow. Freestylers ride up the steep sides of the pipe to pull off amazing aerial tricks. Scores are given for the style, height, and difficulty of the tricks shown.

Dryslope competition

Dryslopes are used where access to snow is limited. In competition, freestylers use ramps to take off and the judging of their tricks is similar to that of halfpipe events.

Major International Competitions

Winter Olympic Games
Held every 4 years with new events to include halfpipe and giant slalom.

ISF World Championships
Held twice a year for the highest ranking riders in halfpipe and slalom events.

ISF Junior World Championships
Held once a year and open to all National Snowboard Association members. Events are for under 16 and 17-18 yr. age groups.

ISF World Series
A series of competitions with slalom and half-pipe events giving riders the chance to build up points to raise their world rankings.

ISF Masters World Cups
Competitions for invited riders only, held three times per year.

Nations' Cup
A team event, open to all nations and including one race and one freestyle event.

Slalom racing

A slalom race, through gates, is against the clock, with the fastest rider winning. In dual slalom, two riders race against each other, and the clock, on parallel courses.

Glossary

When learning to snowboard, or watching boarding events, you may find it helpful to understand the meaning of some of the following words and terms.

A

Air A jump or leap from the ground, usually taking off from a ramp or hit.

B

Backside A term to describe a trick in which the rotation brings the heel edge round first.

Base The bottom surface of a snowboard.

Bindings The devices that clip your boots on to the board.

Boning out Straightening one or other of your legs during a jump.

Bordercross A racing event for at least 4 racers, on a course including slalom-style gates, banked turns, and humps to negotiate.

C

Carve The way an experienced rider uses the shaped edges of the board to make smooth turns that cut into the surface.

D

Dryslope An artificial slope covered in plastic bristles to create a surface on which people can snowboard or ski.

Dual slalom A slalom race event in which the competitors race two at a time on parallel courses.

E

Edging Putting pressure through the working edge of your board.

Extend The action of straightening your legs to lift up from the board.

F

Fakie Riding backwards so that the tail of the board leads.

Fall line An imaginary line that would form the most direct, and therefore steepest, path down a slope.

Flex A term to describe bending the knees and ankles to control the board or absorb the impact of bumps and ridges on the slope.

Freeriding The informal, and non-competitive style of snowboarding for fun, making the most of the natural mountain terrain.

Freestyle The style of snowboarding that incorporates tricks, jumps, and halfpipe riding.

Frontside A term to describe a trick in which the rotation brings the toe edge round first.

G

Gates The coloured posts and panels on a slalom course that mark the route for competitors to follow.

Giant slalom (GS) A slalom race event on a course at least 20 metres wide and with a vertical drop between 120 and 300 metres.

Goofy A term to describe a rider's stance in which the right foot is in the front binding.

Grab To take hold of the snowboard with one or both hands during a jump.

Gradient The steepness of the slope.

H

Halfpipe A U-shaped tube dug into snow for freestyle riding and competition.

Hard boots Rigid boots with a plastic outer shell, usually preferred by racers. The stiffness of the boots helps the rider to transmit body movements to the board.

Heel edge The edge of the board under your heels, regardless of goofy or regular stance.

Hit A bump in the snow, or a jump, from which riders launch themselves.

I

Indy A trick jump in which a grab is made on the toe edge, between the feet, with the back hand.

International Snowboard Federation (ISF) The worldwide governing body of the sport of snowboarding.

L

Leash A safety strap to link the board to the rider to stop it sliding away and being a danger to other slope users.

N

Nose The front end of the snowboard.

Nose slide A ground trick, lifting the tail of the board and sliding on the nose.

O

Ollie A small jump in which the rider springs into the air, using his or her own energy to leave the ground.

R

Ramp A natural, or artificial, slope from which riders can launch into the air.

Regular A term to describe a rider's stance in which the left foot is in the front binding.

S

Sideslip A method of sliding down the slope with the board at 90 degrees to the fall line, and using the uphill edge to control the descent.

Slalom A race event through the gates of a marked course.

Soft boots Flexible lace-up snowboarding boots used by most freestylers and many freeriders.

Step-in boots and bindings An integrated system of boots with metal bails that clip into spring-loaded bindings.

Super G A slalom race event on a course at least 30 metres wide and with a vertical drop between 300 and 500 metres.

T

Tail The back end of the board.

Tail slide A ground trick, lifting the nose of the board and sliding on the tail.

Toe edge The edge under your toes, regardless of your stance.

Traversing Moving diagonally across the slope, using the uphill edge.

W

Warm up Essential preparation before every riding session, to warm and stretch muscles and joints and help prevent injury.

Waist The narrowest part of a snowboard between the nose and tail.

Wax A preparation to apply to the base of a snowboard to help it run smoothly.

Wipe out A spectacular fall.

Index

A
aerial tricks 9, 28, 30, 31, 34
arm guards 32, 33

B
backpack 11
basic riding stance 15
bindings 9, 10, 11, 12, 35
boning out 30, 35
boots 10, 11, 32, 35
bordercross 33, 34, 35
brakes 12, 17, 19, 23, 24, 32
British Snowboarding Association
 (BSA) 37
Burton Carpenter, Jake 9

C
carving turns 26, 27, 35
competitions 9, 32, 33, 34

D
dryslope competition 34, 35
dual slalom 34, 35

E
early boards 9
extending 25

F
fakie backside 180-degree indy 30, 31
fall line 24, 26, 27, 35
falling 14, 22
flexing 25
freeride board 10
freeriding 9, 32, 33, 34, 35
freestyle 9, 28, 29, 30, 31, 32, 33, 35
freestyle board 11

G
getting up 14, 15
giant slalom 33,35
glide 12, 19, 20
gloves 11
goggles 10
goofy stance 11, 35
grabs 30, 35
ground tricks 28, 29

H
halfpipe competition 34, 35
hat 11
hire equipment 10, 16
helmet 32

I
Iguchi, Bryan 8
injury, avoiding 14, 15, 16, 32
International Snowboarding
 Federation (ISF) 34, 35, 37
ISF Junior World Championships 34
ISF Masters World Cups 34
ISF World Championships 34
ISF World Series 34

J
jackets 11
jump turns 16
jumps 30, 31

L
leash, safety 10, 12, 35
leg guards 32, 33
linking turns 24, 25, 27

N
Nations' Cup 34
neutral stance 15, 18, 19, 22
nose slide 28, 29, 35

O
ollie 30, 31, 35
Olympic competition 34

P
Poppen, Sherman 9

R
race board 10, 11, 32
racing 9, 32, 33, 34
regular stance 11, 35
riding fakie 18, 19, 20, 21, 28, 30, 31

S
scooting 12
sideslipping 18, 19, 35
Sims, Tom 9
slalom gates 9, 32, 33, 34, 35
slalom racing 32, 33, 34, 35
snurfer 9
soft boots 11, 35
spins 28, 29, 30, 31
step-in bindings 11, 35
stomp pad 12, 35
stretching 16, 17
suncreams 10
sunglasses 10
super G 33, 35

T
tail slide 28, 29, 35
toe edge 17, 35
toolkit 11
traversing 20, 21, 35
trousers 10
turns 22, 23, 24, 25, 26, 27

W
walking uphill 12, 13
warming up 16, 17, 35
wax 11, 32, 35

Useful addresses

Here are the addresses of some snowboarding organizations, which you may find useful.

British Snowboarding Association (BSA)
5 Cressex Road,
High Wycombe,
Buckinghamshire
HP12 4PG   Tel/Fax : 01494 462225

BSA English Office
134 Coney Green Drive,
Northfield, Birmingham
B31 4EJ   Tel/Fax 0121 4779001

BSA Welsh Office
326 Middle Road,
Gendros,
Swansea
SA5 8EW   Tel/Fax: 01792 585080

BSA Irish Office (N. Ireland and Eire)
75 Marsham Court
Kilmacud,
County Dublin,
Eire   Tel/Fax: 00 353 1 283 6771

BSA Scottish Office
9 Winton Terrace,
Edinburgh,
EH10 7AP   Tel/Fax 0131 445 4046

International Snowboard Federation (ISF)
Pradlerstrasse 21,
A-6020 Innsbruck,
Austria   Tel: 00 43 512 342834
               Fax: 00 43 512 3428342

Snowboard Australia
PO Box 256,
Falls Creek,
Victoria 3699   Tel/Fax: 03 5758 3653

New Zealand Snowboard Association
PO Box 27501
Wellington
New Zealand   Fax: 04 499 8136

Rachel   Arash   Kate   Tariq   Ryan

Acknowledgments

Dorling Kindersley would like to thank the following people
for their help in the production of this book:

Steve Davis, for his technical advice and help in setting up the photography shoots; all the young snowboarders for their patience and enthusiasm during the photographic sessions; 1-2-Freeride, Radair, Nice, and Burton for the equipment loaned; Nicholas Hewetson for diagrammatic illustrations; Almudena Díaz for DTP design; Patricia Grogan for additional editorial assistance; Joanna Malivoire for additional design assistance; and Sophia Tampakopoulos for the jacket design.

Picture credits
key: b=bottom; l=left; r=right; c=centre; t=top.

Allsport: Antow Want 9cl/ Mike Cooper 32br.
AppalSport: Allan Green 34tr/Sang Tan 9bl, 34br/Stig 9bc, 33tr.
Burton Snowboards: 9tl, team rider Bryan Iguchi 8tl/Richard Walsh, team rider Peter Bauer 34cr/Jon Foster, team rider Terje Haakonsen 25cr, team rider Nicolas Conte 27bl.
Jonno Gibbins: 23tr.
Lee Irvine: 10bl, 34bl, 34cr.
John Layshock: 8br, 8cl, 8bl, back jacket br, inside back jacket t.
Sims Sports: 9c.
Jess Stock/Stock Shot: 21tr, 22bl, 34tr, 30tr, endpapers.